DETECTIVE ACADEMY ™

D0480147

Crime Scene Investigation

by **Paul Mauro**
with **H. Keith Melton**
consultant

Scholastic Inc.
New York • Toronto • London • Auckland • Sydney
Mexico City • New Delhi • Hong Kong • Buenos Aires

ISBN: 0-439-57175-8

Design: Mark Neston

Illustrations: Daniel Aycock, Yancey Labat, Antoine Clarke

Photos: Mark Neston, Daniel Aycock, Lightning Powder Company (pgs. 21 and 29), dispatcher photo (pg. 6) courtesy of the New York Police Department.

A special thanks to Officer Tim Duffy of the 6th Precinct of the New York Police Department, and to Police Officer Emma Llaurado and Sergeant Rick Lopez for the photos on pages 4, 6, and 7; and to CSI Technician David Sentowski on pages 42 and 43.

12 11 10 9 8 7 6 5 4 3 2   6 7 8/0

Printed in the U.S.A.

First Scholastic printing, October 2003

The publisher has made every effort to ensure that the activities in this book are safe when done as instructed. Children are encouraged to do their detective activities with willing friends and family members and to respect others' right to privacy. Adults should provide guidance and supervision whenever the activity requires.

Case Log

Case File

DA When you see this symbol throughout the book, you'll know to use your **detective equipment** in the activity.

When you see this symbol throughout the book, you'll know there's a related activity to be found on the Detective Academy **website**.

Scene of the Crime

Welcome back, rookie detective! You know, part of learning to be a great detective is knowing how to think in a new way. Detectives spend most of their time thinking in reverse, trying to learn about something that's already happened (in this case, a crime). They look at the place where a crime occurred, and ask themselves: What happened here? And who was here at the time it happened? Detectives have to use their brains to travel back in time and "see" everything the criminal is trying to keep hidden!

Usually, the detective's search into the past will start right where the crime happened: at the **crime scene**. The crime scene usually holds enough evidence to launch the detective on his journey back in time. Along with other special members of the police force, who have specific investigative skills (you'll be meeting them shortly), detectives carefully examine the crime scene and discover clues an untrained person doesn't see (it's like having X-ray vision!).

But you know what? It's *not* X-ray vision. A detective looks into the past using skills he's *learned*. Skills like his powers of observation and deductive reasoning, his memory, his knowledge of special equipment—all skills *you* began to learn in your Detective Academy *Basic Training Manual*.

Patrol officers like Emma Llaurado are usually the first responders at crime scenes.

In this book, you'll learn the specific techniques of **crime scene investigation**. At the scene of a crime, detectives go over every inch of the immediate area, uncovering all the evidence that's there. They then test that evidence to see who it points to as the **perpetrator** of the crime. How detectives manage to work this magic is what crime scene investigation (CSI for short) is all about—and what you'll be learning in the activities coming up!

THE SCENE TEAM!

No matter how skilled a detective is, working a crime scene is a pretty big job—after all, so much of what you need to solve the case is right there! For that reason, detectives *never* handle the crime scene alone. In fact, detectives aren't usually even the first members of the police department who get to a crime scene. **First responders**, the uniformed police officers on **patrol**, usually arrive at a crime scene before anyone else (we'll see how, coming up!).

CSI technicians drive vans like this one when they go to crime scenes—they've got a lot of special equipment to take along!

Because they're the first arrivals, first responders have lots to do—but once their work is done and the investigation is ready to start, they get on their two-way radios and call the detective: that's you, rookie!

As the detective "working" a crime scene, you'll, in turn, be able to call for help, just as the first responder called for you! **Crime scene investigation (CSI) technicians**, who are members of the police force with special training in science, will help you gather evidence at the scene. **Forensic scientists** then test the evidence in a lab, to see if it's useful in solving the crime. But remember, even though you get help, *you*, the detective, are still the head of the team—the **lead investigator**. It's *your* job to direct those other police unit helpers and to use their work to help you build your case—and to catch the perpetrator of the crime!

DA Detective Equipment

A big part of investigating crime scenes is using specialized equipment to gather and analyze evidence. This equipment helps investigators make sure no clue—no matter how small!—is overlooked. This month's crime scene investigation gear includes:

- **UV Powder**, which will help you bring to life **fingerprint** clues you didn't even know were there.

- **UV Light**, which you'll use with the UV powder to discover the toughest-to-find prints.

- **Print Brush** to help you apply the UV powder and find fingerprints on various surfaces.

- **Shoe Covers** to help you keep your crime scenes protected and uncontaminated.

- **Crime Scene Tape** to rope off your crime scenes to keep them undisturbed and the evidence exactly as it was found.

CRIME SCENE DO NOT ENTER

Detective Academy Website

Want to learn more about crime scene investigation? Want to practice your crime scene skills? Then get online at **www.scholastic.com/detective**. This month's password is: **crimescene**. Remember, every month you'll find a new password to give you access to the Detective Academy website—and even more ways to build your detective skills!

PASSWORD: CRIMESCENE

Working the Crime Scene: From Start to Finish

START HERE

12:45 P.M.: 911 CALL TO EMERGENCY DISPATCHER

A woman returns home from work on her lunch hour to discover that her house has been burglarized and dials 9-1-1 for the police.

4:47 P.M.: CSI SENDS EVIDENCE TO THE POLICE LABORATORY

Crime scene investigators send the evidence they've gathered to the special police lab, where it will be tested by forensic scientists—members of the police department who specialize in scientifically analyzing evidence. They use the latest equipment and technology to determine what crime scene evidence is valuable to the investigation (Is it a clue? Science will tell!). Eventually, the police lab will send the detective a report on the results of their tests. If it's important evidence, the detective can use it to help build his case. The crime scene processing is complete—but the case is still in progress!

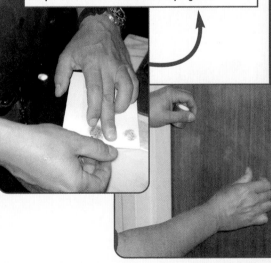

2:50 P.M.: CRIME SCENE INVESTIGATION TECHNICIANS ARRIVE

CSI technicians arrive and begin to search every inch of the crime scene. The evidence will be analyzed and passed on to the detective so he can solve the case!

12:46 P.M.: EMERGENCY DISPATCHER RADIOS PATROL OFFICERS TO RESPOND

The emergency dispatcher uses a special two-way radio to tell first responder patrol officers that there's been a burglary in their area.

12:53 P.M.: FIRST RESPONDERS ARRIVE AT THE SCENE

First responder patrol officers arrive at the scene, provide immediate assistance, and make sure everyone is safe.

1:21 P.M.: FIRST RESPONDERS REQUEST A DETECTIVE

Once everything at the crime scene is safe and secure, patrol officers radio for a detective to respond. The investigation is about to begin!

CRIME SCENE DO NOT ENTER

2:10 P.M.: DETECTIVE REQUESTS CSI TO RESPOND

In order to properly work this crime scene, the detective calls in the crime scene investigation unit!

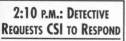

1:38 P.M.: THE DETECTIVE ARRIVES AND BEGINS THE INVESTIGATION

The detective arrives to check out the crime scene. What is the nature and extent of the burglary? Are there any witnesses? Will he (the detective) have to call for additional help? Questions, questions, questions...!

FIRST RESPONDERS: A DETECTIVE'S TEAMMATES

A detective working a case is constantly asking himself (or herself) questions about the past. To a detective, life can be like one long history test! And *you* thought history just happened in class!

Fortunately, detectives don't have to take this test alone. They get lots of help from their teammates "on the job" (that is, at the police department). When working a **crime scene**, that first help a detective gets is from **first responders**—the police officers who "respond first" to an emergency call of a crime. Once first responders get there, almost *everything* they do will affect what the crime scene looks like when you, the detective, catch the case.

So how *do* first responders get there first, you ask? Good question! Imagine you're walking down a street with lots of stores and businesses. It's dark out and most of the shops have closed—there's nobody around. Suddenly, turning the corner, you notice a man with a big set of clippers trying to cut the chain on an expensive mountain bike that's locked to a bike rack. Hey, wait a second. You *know* that bicycle. Doesn't it belong to a friend of yours? You back away slowly, without being noticed. You realize—you're witnessing a crime!

You head right for the nearest pay phone and dial 9-1-1. (Tip: It's free to call the police from most pay phones and cell phones.) A woman answers your call by saying, "**Emergency dispatcher**, what's your emergency?" You tell her what you just saw. Meanwhile, the bicycle thief is frantically yanking on that stubborn bike chain.

Now every second counts. If the dispatcher doesn't get your info to the police right away, your friend is going to lose his means of transportation! So the emergency dispatcher springs into action. She uses a special two-way radio to contact the police units that are patrolling in your area. As she does, she knows her message to the police needs to be fast—so she keeps it as short as possible. But, at the same time, she needs to be accurate, and give lots of info, too. How is she going to manage all that?

Codes, that's how!

POLICE HAVE THEIR OWN LANGUAGE!

Well, maybe not a *whole* language. But when police speak to emergency dispatchers—or each other—over their portable radios, they use a special code filled with lots of numbers. To an outsider, a police radio might *sound* like the world's longest and hardest math problem ("10-35, 10-98, 10-4!"). But to the police, these codes tell a whole story—and fast.

To get you thinking like a detective, here's a list of commonly used police codes. What do you notice about the two lists of numbers? Is there a relationship between the numbers on the left and those on the right?

Crimes In Progress		Crimes In the Past
10-35	Robbery	10-25
10-36	Burglary	10-26
10-37	Assault	10-27
10-38	Vehicle Theft	10-28
10-39	Vehicle Accident	10-29

If you figured out that the numbers for the "in progress" crimes (10-35, 10-36, 10-37—on the left) are all exactly *ten higher* than the "in the past" codes (10-25, 10-26, 10-27—on the right), you've taken your first step in talking the talk of the police!

First responders listening to the emergency dispatcher on their radios can always tell that a crime in the "thirties" (like a 10-36) is *in progress*—it's happening right now! A crime in the "twenties" is *in the past*—it's *already* happened. When you see police cars with their sirens blaring and their lights flashing, they're rushing to a crime in progress. Here's another question for you, rookie: Of the two sets of codes, the "thirties" or the "twenties"—which do you think a detective deals with most? See *Case Closed* for the answer.

But describing crimes is not *all* that police codes are used for. For instance, there are codes that describe where the criminal, or **perpetrator**, is:

10-87—The perpetrator has left the scene.
10-97—The perpetrator is still on the scene.

There are also radio codes that police officers use when they need assistance. For instance:

10-88—I need help, but don't rush.
10-98—I need help right now!

Sometimes, the police also use coded words instead of numbers. For instance:

roll a bus	Send an ambulance.
perp	A perpetrator.
one under	A perpetrator under arrest.
descrip	Description (usually of a perpetrator).
vic	Short for victim.
Central	Short for "emergency dispatcher."
Unit to advise?	Is there a police unit in the area to check out the scene?

And finally, most police radio transmissions end with the famous:

10-4—I heard you, I understand.

DETECTIVE JARGON

When you see a word or phrase in boldface throughout the book, check here to see what it means!

Assault: When a perpetrator physically attacks another person.

Burglary: When a perpertrator breaks in somewhere with the intent to steal—whether he *does* steal anything or not doesn't matter, it's still a burglary.

Crime Scene: The area where a crime was committed, like the apartment building where someone was robbed.

Crime Scene Investigation (CSI): The process of collecting and analyzing the evidence discovered at the scene of a crime.

Crime Scene Investigation (CSI) Technician: A member of the police department whose job it is to collect evidence at the scene of a crime.

Crime Scene Notification: A sign that police post to warn onlookers that a certain area is a crime scene, and that they must not enter.

Emergency Dispatcher: The person who answers emergency 9-1-1 calls and sends out police officers.

Fingerprints: An impression on a surface made by the ridges on fingertips.

First Responder: A uniformed police officer who is the first one to arrive at a crime scene. Also known as a "patrol officer."

Forensic Science: The use of scientific principles, mostly of biology and chemistry, to analyze evidence from a crime.

Forensic Scientist: A person trained in using biology, chemistry, and other sciences to analyze the evidence from a crime.

Lead Investigator: The detective in charge of a particular case.

Partial: A piece or part of a fingerprint. A partial can sometimes be used for identification, if enough of the full fingerprint is present.

Patrol: A police officer is on patrol when he is out and about, protecting the streets from crime.

Perpetrator: A person who commits a crime (sometimes abbreviated as *perp*).

Robbery: When a perpetrator steals someone else's property using violence or intimidation.

Theft: When a perpetrator steals someone else's property *without* using violence or intimidation— he steals without being seen or noticed by the victim.

Theory: An idea that a detective has about a possible way a crime was committed.

Tool Marks: Scrapes and scratches left by a tool on an area—usually a window or door lock— that indicate someone was trying to break in.

Trace Evidence: Tiny pieces of evidence, like hair, fiber, and dust, found at a crime scene.

Ultraviolet (UV): When you use UV light, it causes certain objects to glow, making them easier to see.

Vehicle Accident: When someone gets into an accident, or crash, while in their car, van, or on their bike.

Vehicle Theft: The act of stealing someone's car, van, bike, or other vehicle.

Radio Active!

The key to learning police codes is simple: practice, practice, practice. Because they use codes every day, police officers sometimes use them without even realizing it! Detectives, too, use radio codes—even when they're just talking to each other, and not on the radio! That shows you what a big part of police life radio codes occupy. They're like a secret language that police officers keep all to themselves!

But now that you've learned some real police codes (on page 9), how about practicing this secret language a bit?

What You Do

Part I. By the Numbers

1. Invite a friend over to help you memorize the "in progress" radio codes (the "thirties") from page 9. Can you remember what number a **robbery** in progress is? What's a 10-37?

2. Once you've got a pretty good feel for the in-progress list, move on to the "past" list. Remember, the past numbers are the same as the in-progress codes, except they are in the *twenties*, not the *thirties*. This should help (in fact, that's why most police departments set it up that way—to make the codes easier to remember!). Have your friend test you.

3. Now turn back to the coded *words*, also on page 9. See how many you can commit to memory.

Part II. Translation Time!

Got all the codes down cold? Okay, then, rookie, see how you do on these transmissions. Check out *Case Closed* for the translations!

1. "Central, we've got a 10-39 here, corner of Broadway and Canal. Two injuries, not life threatening. Roll me a bus." Write your translation of this transmission in your detective notebook.

2. Now try this one: "Units, I've got a call of a 10-25 at 325 Owen Avenue. Caller states **perp** is 10-87. Unit in the area to advise?" Once you've uncoded the message, ask yourself this: Is that a police officer speaking, or is it an **emergency dispatcher**?

3. Here's another. "Receiving a call of a 10-38, East 10th Street and Nicholls Boulevard. Caller states perp is still 10-97. Repeat, perp is 97 on this 10-38. Unit available to respond?"

Part III. A 10-36 With a 10-98!

If you think you've got the hang of it, then let's keep going. You're working in your office at police headquarters when suddenly you hear the following transmission from a police radio (most detectives keep a police radio nearby to hear what the **first responders** are up to). This is an actual radio transmission from the New York City Police Department. The conversations are between the emergency dispatcher and first responder police officers. Can you and your friend tell what's going on?

Transmission

Dispatcher: *Units, I'm receiving a call of a 10-36. A 10-36 at 425 North 47th Street, Apartment 4-B. Caller states perp is a white male, approximately 35, wearing blue jeans, black jacket, backward baseball cap. Caller states he returned to his apartment and* found perp in kitchen. Perp threatened him. No information on any possible weapons. Perp is 10-97. Repeat, perp is 97.

Police Officer #1: 10-4, Central. I'll respond. Can you 10-88 me another unit? 88 me a unit to that location, Central.

Dispatcher: 10-4.

Police Officer #2: *Central, I'm already at the location of that 10-36. Better roll a bus here, Central. Vic is an elderly male, and perp startled him. Want to make sure vic is okay. Be advised perp is 10-87 at this time. Perp fled through kitchen window.*

Dispatcher: *10-4. Bus to your location. Units, perp is 10-87 at this time. Stand by for repeat descrip. Perp is a male white, approximately 35 years of age, wearing a—*

Police Officer #1: *I've got him spotted, Central! Perp just jumped off the fire escape and is fleeing northbound on Eighth Avenue! North on Eighth Avenue. Foot pursuit, Central! 10-98! 10-98!*

What's the Real Deal?

You may have noticed that all police codes have a "10" before them. This helps distinguish them from *other* numbers the dispatcher may say on the radio (like an address, for instance). The "10" also helps keep all the police codes separated when the dispatcher says a few of them in a row—sort of the way a series of commas work in a sentence!

The two-way radios police officers use are getting their batteries charged here.

Without codes, talking on the radio would be much more confusing and time-consuming for police. The codes get across a lot of info fast—even in stressful situations (which police encounter pretty regularly, you know!). Radio codes are so important, in fact, that they're one of the first things a new police officer learns when he joins the department.

Respond...and React!

As you've seen by now, **first responders** have a tough job! Because they're the first police officers to arrive at the scene of a crime, they have a whole list of important stuff to do—and sometimes they don't have a lot of time in which to do it. So they have to think—and act—fast! There are specific rules first responders must follow, and they get to know the rules so well that they can follow them automatically!

Because detectives *start out* as first responders, they also know these rules by heart. Which means you should, too!

What You Do

Part I. Check Yourself!

Check out this checklist to see how the first responder to a **crime scene** knows what to do.

FIRST RESPONDER CHECKLIST

☑ **Ensure the safety of everyone involved.** If the **perpetrator** is still at the **crime scene**, arrest him so he can't do any more harm. If he's not still on the scene (or even if he is), but someone is hurt, get an ambulance there right away—even if it means the perp gets away!

☑ **Get the story.** Find out what happened. Talk to the victim, witnesses—anybody who can shed light on the situation.

☑ **Get on the radio and ask for help.** Tell Central what you need—more police at the scene, reinforcements to chase a fleeing perpetrator—whatever it is, get the word out!

☑ **Secure the crime scene.** Make sure the scene—and the evidence in it—stays undisturbed until a detective arrives.

☑ **Notify a detective.** When the emergency is over and the perpetrator is gone, it's time to hand the scene over to a detective so that the investigation can begin. (Of course, if you've caught the perpetrator on the scene, you don't need to call a detective. You've already got your man—or woman.)

Part II. It's All In the Timing!

Got a feel for it? See how well you can do as the first responder on a couple of crime scenes that are the same...but sort of different.

On the next page are three crime scenes based on the radio transmission from *Case File #1: Radio Active! Part III*. You might want to go back and read through it again, to refresh your memory. All three pictures are of the same crime scene; however, each picture shows you—the first responder—the scene as if you were arriving at a different *time*. As the first responder, what will each scene require? Using your first responder checklist, decide what you will do at each scene, in the order in which you will do them. Then compare your answers with those in *Case Closed* and see how you did!

What Would a First Responder Do At the Scene of This Burglary?

Picture #1:

As a first responder, what would you do first in this scene? What would you do next?

Picture #2:

What would you do first here?

This is the same setting as the first picture, but not quite the same scene. What's different? What's your first move?

Picture #3:

What would you do at *this* scene?

Hint: This is far more than an empty room!

More From Detective Squad

Want some more practice as a first responder? Log on to **www.scholastic.com/detective** for a fast-action simulation!

What's the Real Deal?

Even though they're not detectives yet, first responders are the backbone of every police department. They're the uniformed police officers who "chase trouble"—who race to the scene of crimes in progress, usually without knowing exactly what they're getting into.

Not only do first responders sometimes have to make life-and-death decisions, they're also responsible for making sure that the crime scene isn't disturbed, so that the detective can start investigating if the perpetrator got away.

Responding to a crime scene in a specific way, as you did in this activity, ensures that first responders will make the best decisions to stop the perpetrator, help the victims, and protect the crime scene.

They may not be ranked as detectives or supervisors, but all police work starts with first responders!

CASE IN POINT The Incredible Exploding...Dye Pack!

In order to foil bank robbers, many banks use "exploding dye packs"—special stacks of dollar bills banded together with a tiny explosive charge hidden inside them. The charge is surrounded by red dye, so that when the robber *thinks* he has gotten away with the money—bang! He's suddenly covered in red ink, making him easy for police to spot!

In March of 2003, first responders with the Columbus Police Department in Ohio rushed to the scene of a robbery at the National City Bank in Columbus's busy downtown section. About a block away from the bank, the officers noticed a man walking kind of strangely. Even though he had no ink on him, they decided to check him out—and ended up making an arrest!

It turns out that after fleeing with the money, the perpetrator decided to hide the bills—by putting them in his pants pocket...which is where the money was when the dye pack exploded!

The perpetrator was charged with robbery—and sharp-eyed first responders ended up with an excellent arrest!

Secure That Scene! 🔒

Stuff You'll Need

- Crime scene tape 🛡
- Around ten pennies
- Ruler
- Scissors
- Some paper
- Masking tape
- Rookie friends

Want to know one of the hidden rules of crime scenes that all first responders know? It's this: Crime scenes draw crowds! Whether it's passersby on the street, nosy neighbors, TV and newspaper reporters, or just extra police officers showing up to lend a hand—before you know it, crime scenes can start to look like someone's giving away free pizza!

For a detective, a crowded crime scene can be a nightmare. That's because a case can become difficult to solve when valuable evidence is lost or trampled. So when first responders get there, one of their most important tasks is to secure the scene. That means, besides making sure that no one is hurt and eliminating any threats, they take steps to protect the scene—so that the evidence is preserved exactly as it was found and is in good shape when the detective arrives.

So how *do* first responders secure the scene with so many people around? Let's find out!

What You Do

Part I. Protect That Evidence

1. You're the first responder on the scene of that 10-36 in *Case File #1: Radio Active! Part III* (see page 12). Using your crime scene tape, rope off an area in your kitchen around a window (just make sure no senior detectives are cooking dinner at the time!). If your kitchen is too busy, you can always use your room, or another quiet area. Tie the crime scene tape to anything handy, just like real police do. Just make sure it stays in place!

2. Next, set up the crime scene—inside the roped-off area you just made—as it was in that 10-36 (use the pictures on page 14). Place your pennies about eight inches apart on the floor, leading to the window—they make your blood trail. Then use your scissors to cut pieces of paper

(your broken glass) into various shapes, from about two inches across to about a ½ inch across. Scatter this paper around the floor near the window.

3. Open a few of your kitchen cabinets and drawers (or other drawers if you're not in your kitchen). Now, using the masking tape, make an X on the floor inside the roped off area near the entrance to your kitchen. This marks where the victim was when the perpetrator came through the window. Put another taped X on the floor a few feet from the window, and near some kitchen cabinets or the refrigerator—this marks how far the perpetrator got into the room before he was spotted by the victim and fled.

4. Congratulations! You've just recreated a pretty realistic crime scene! What's more, using your crime scene tape, you've secured (or protected) the scene as well. Now that that's done, take the next step to prepare for when the detective arrives.

Part II. Get the Story

1. Invite over some rookie friends to see if they can figure out what happened in the

crime scene you just set up. Show them the blood trail and the broken glass. Then ask them: What do you think these X's on the floor indicate?

2. If they can't figure it out, tell them to take a close look at the open kitchen drawers and cabinets. Do they help as clues?

3. Once your fellow rookies know what happened at the scene of this crime, discuss where you've put up your crime scene tape. Did you include the *whole* crime scene? Is there any evidence that could be found outside the crime scene area?

4. Have each of your fellow rookies imagine that *they* are the first responder assigned to this incident. Ask them: what do *you* think you should do first? Check *Case Closed* for the answer!

Tip:
It's always better to rope your crime scene off on the big side, rather than the small. That way, you're less likely to miss something important.

What's the Real Deal?

Just like the crime scene you set up in *Part I*, real detectives often set up imitation crime scenes themselves when they're working on a case. With the model crime scene, they can examine the evidence and test out a **theory** of what happened to help them solve the crime (you'll learn more about this in *Case File # 10: Testing: One, Two, Three*). Detectives also draw diagrams, build models, and even act out crimes, all so they can "see" the scene better. Sometimes, to catch a criminal, you've got to imagine you are one yourself!

Have a look at *Case in Point* on this page for an eerie way that detectives sometimes get their crime scene training!

CASE IN POINT
Child's Play? Not Exactly!

The latest tool for teaching the techniques of crime scene investigation is…dollhouses?

As a way to interest college students in **forensic science**, a professor at the University of Maryland has designed a number of miniature, carefully constructed dollhouses for use as a teaching aid. But instead of filling the houses with dolls, the professor fills them with crime scenes!

Professor Thomas P. Mauriello uses the dollhouses to show students miniature versions of crime scenes involving **burglaries**, **robberies**, and accidents. After learning about some of the techniques that investigators use, students are then invited to use this new knowledge to figure out what occurred at each scene. Much like you're asked to do in this book!

Here's a "robbery" crime scene in a dollhouse set up.
Can you tell what's happening here?

Read the Fine Prints!

Stuff You'll Need
- UV powder DA
- Print brush DA
- UV light DA
- Scotch tape
- Index cards
- A rookie friend
- A cloth or paper towel
- Various objects in your room
- Plastic gloves

As you learned in your *Basic Training Manual*, one of the best pieces of evidence at a **crime scene** is **fingerprints**. If a detective can find prints at the scene, he can then match those prints to a **perpetrator** whose fingerprints are on file. Now he knows who's been at the crime scene—even if they're long gone!

Fingerprints can often be found on smooth objects like drinking glasses, bottles, shiny metals, and windows. Sometimes, they can even be found by just looking in the right places, or using a magnifying glass. Unfortunately, criminals are not always cooperative enough to leave these nice, visible prints. So how *do* **CSI technicians** find fingerprints that aren't visible to the naked eye? **UV** powder, of course!

When fingerprints are left on surfaces that make them hard to see—like cloth or paper, for instance—they are discovered or *raised* by covering them with a special powder that makes them visible. And when **crime scene investigators** need to find fingerprints that are very, *very* faint, they use UV powder because it glows when a special light is shined on them.

But just *seeing* fingerprints isn't enough—CSI techs need to *save* them! In order to hang on to a fingerprint they discover (and so record a permanent record of it), CSI techs need to "lift" the print. This means that after they brush on fingerprint powder, they press a special tape onto the print that the fingerprint sticks to. This tape is then lifted, and the print can be stored, filed, matched to other prints, and even photographed and run through a computer to look for a match.

Fingerprinting is one of the most important skills a CSI tech learns, and one of the best pieces of evidence for a detective on a case. Want to see how it works?

What You Do

Part I. Light It Up!

Some prints you can see with the naked eye, but others need help to be seen...that's where your UV powder and light come in handy!

1. First, let's hunt down some visible prints. Get up close to your television set (make sure the set's turned off!). Do you see any prints? Place your fingers against the screen, then remove them. Do you see the marks your fingers left?

2. Try the same thing on your window. Make sure you have good light. Try tilting your head to look from different angles. Do you see any prints others have left? Concentrate on the areas around the edges of the window, where people tend to touch it.

3. Now open your jar of UV powder. Take your print brush and dip it in the powder. Using *very light strokes* of the brush, apply the powder *very thinly* over the area where you want to take fingerprints off the window. A soft and light dusting is key; too much powder, and all you'll see is green!

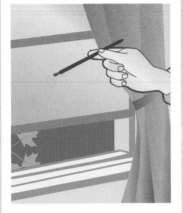

4. Once you've dusted the area, pick up your UV light and squeeze it between your fingers to turn it on. Shine the UV light over the area you've just dusted. Now can you see the prints? (If you saw *some* before, you should see even more now!)

5. Once you've gotten the hang of raising or discovering some prints this way, try it on some of the other surfaces that you know show prints well (like glasses and mirrors).

Part II. Digging Deeper

Once you've practiced with the easy-to-find print surfaces, it's time to step it up a bit!

1. Find a smooth, flat surface that isn't made of glass—the top of your desk or dresser will do, or maybe even a book on a shelf. Make sure you can't see any prints on it with your naked eye. Now, using the same technique you used in *Part I*, dust that surface for prints—then shine your UV light on them to make them visible.

2. Try a few different surfaces—your curtains, your closet door, a magazine cover, a video game player...anywhere and anything a burglar might touch while looking through your stuff! Here's a tip: If you think you've used too much powder while you're printing, don't brush it off—*blow* it off with *very soft* puffs of breath. This will make sure you don't wipe that hard-to-find print away while trying to remove the excess dust! Fingerprinting is like any other skill—it takes practice! So keep at it—even experienced techs might only find one or two good samples on these hard-to-fingerprint surfaces!

Part III. Give Me a Lift

Now that you've practiced dusting for prints, you need to learn that other trick of the trade: *lifting* prints.

1. Take a piece of scotch tape and carefully press it on top of one of the prints you just dusted in *Part I* or *II*.

2. Rub the tape to be sure it makes contact evenly over the surface of the print. But be sure not to move the tape once you've placed it on the print.

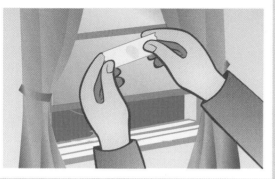

3. Now, carefully pull the tape up off the dusted print. Place the tape on an index card. Can you still see the print you found? Even if you only got a **partial** (a part of the fingerprint), you now have a permanent record of that fingerprint!

Part IV. Print Hunt!

A big part of getting good prints to use as evidence is *finding* them in the first place. Try this, to see how your print-hunting abilities stack up!

1. First, invite a fellow rookie over for some fingerprint training.

2. Have your friend wait outside the room as you set up your crime scene in your kitchen again, just like you had it for *Case File #3: Secure That Scene!* (remember to get a senior detective's permission first!).

3. Once you have it set up, go around the scene and wipe down every surface you can, so that it's free of prints. Make sure the glasses, the refrigerator, the tabletop, and the cabinets are all wiped clean with a damp cloth or paper towel.

4. Next, purposely leave *your* prints on three surfaces: one easy one (like a drinking glass or the window), one a bit harder (try your refrigerator door or a plastic placemat) and one really hard one (on your wooden cabinets or the window curtains). Tell your fellow rookie that you've left three of your prints on three *visible* areas around the room, and ask her to find them, using the techniques you learned in *Parts I, II,* and *III*. She should wear plastic gloves while she hunts to make sure she doesn't mix her own prints with yours!

5. Now reverse roles, and see if you can find her left-behind prints!

JUST THE FACTS

All the Colors of the Rainbow

Because powder is used to make hard-to-find fingerprints show themselves, it sometimes helps to see the prints if the powder has some *color* to it — like the green powder you got in your equipment kit. CSI technicians generally choose a powder color that is the *opposite* of the surface they're looking for fingerprints on. This helps the print show up even more clearly. For example, if you were looking for prints on a black surface, you would use a light-colored fingerprint powder, like white, green, or pink. Fingerprint powders come in many different colors — black, yellow, orange, pink, blue, and so on — because surfaces do, too!

More From Detective Squad

Get on-line at **www.scholastic.com/detective** for some more practice with UV.

What's the Real Deal?

Fingerprinting is one of the oldest techniques in **forensic science**—detectives have been relying on prints for over 100 years. And with good reason. Fingerprints are very valuable pieces of evidence when hunting the perpetrator of a crime. Of all the skills a CSI technician can learn, fingerprinting is among the most valuable!

As you probably learned during this activity, good prints aren't always easy to come by. Perpetrators don't always help out by touching the best surfaces—so the practice of using powder to find fingerprints came into use. When you touch something, the sweat and oils from your skin sticks to surfaces. Fingerprint powder itself sticks to this sweat and oil. And so, instead of invisible sweat...we see a dusty fingerprint!

But even good fingerprints aren't always valuable evidence. Remember, prints are only good if we can "match" them to a perpetrator (that is, find a perpetrator's prints that are on file that the new prints resemble). If the perpetrator of a crime has never been fingerprinted and his prints aren't on file, even good prints are nothing more than...sweat, oil, and dust.

CASE IN POINT The Polite Burglar

In 2001, New York City detectives were investigating a series of burglaries committed by a perpetrator nobody had seen—until he made a mistake and met two of his victims face-to-face!

The perpetrator had been targeting very expensive apartments in a rich area and always struck when no one was home. So when an elderly couple walked in on him as he was going through their belongings, he was as surprised as they were!

The elderly couple later described the burglar as "extremely polite." (He even apologized for stealing from them!) But after the perpetrator fled the scene and the couple went to call the police, they discovered something—their phone was missing! It was this perpetrator's routine to pull the phone from the wall and hide it, so that even after his victims discovered their home had been burglarized, they couldn't call the police. It was a clever idea—and also his biggest mistake.

CSI techs dusted the whole apartment (including the couple's safe), but found no prints—until the victims mentioned having to use the neighbor's phone to call the police. That's when the techs searched for and found the telephone in a dumpster in front of the building. And on the phone they found—one fingerprint!

It was enough. Detectives managed to match the print to a perpetrator who had been arrested before. When they tracked him down, they discovered evidence of at least 10 other burglaries he'd committed!

HOLLYWOOD IT'S NOT!

But It's Getting There!

In the old days, Hollywood had almost no clue about how police and detectives actually did their jobs. On most old detective shows, for example, a detective looking for fingerprints at a crime scene would often use a handkerchief to pick up a drinking glass or similar object—and in the process, wipe off any prints that might have been there!

These days, Hollywood has gotten much better at showing detective work accurately. Yes, sometimes they still do "stretch" things a bit—for instance, shows like *CSI* and *CSI Miami* often have a single actor portray a combination detective, CSI technician, and forensic scientist all in one (and you, rookie, know that isn't the way real detectives work!). And in most movies, detectives engage in shootouts and car chases on what seems like a daily basis! In reality, detective work is much less violent. Detectives rarely fire their weapons, and they almost never engage in car chases. Remember, detectives work *after* the crime's been committed—they spend most of their time talking to witnesses and examining evidence.

But overall, Hollywood has worked hard to improve the accuracy of TV and movies. For example, the popular TV series *NYPD Blue* and *Dragnet* hire actual police officers to tell them what the "real deal" is. And the long-running series *Law & Order* not only works with the police department to keep the show accurate—it actually hires real police officers to act on the show!

Top to bottom: Scenes from *NYPD Blue*, *Law & Order*, and *Dragnet*

Without a Trace?
I Don't Think So!

Stuff You'll Need
- Two pairs of clean, white socks
- Magnifying glass DA
- Tape
- Pair of shoes
- A rookie friend

Do you have a pet dog or cat? Have you ever noticed what your furry pal looks like after she runs through the woods or plays in the street? Half the outside world ends up in her fur, doesn't it? Which then ends up on your living room rug!

Well believe it or not, *you* aren't all that different from your pet! *You* also pick up bits of grass, dirt, or other tiny stuff from outside as you go through your day. And in the same way that your pet tends to leave hair all over the house, you leave evidence of yourself as well! And guess who *else* leaves bits of themselves around? That's right—**perpetrators**.

When a detective arrives at a **crime scene**, some of the best evidence on hand isn't often immediately visible. But by careful examination—and using special equipment—detectives and **CSI technicians** are often able to find important **trace evidence**. These clues include hair, clothing threads, dirt smudges, and other tiny stuff that the perpetrator left at the scene. Detectives gather this evidence, then send it to a sophisticated crime laboratory to be analyzed by **forensic scientists**. By matching this evidence to the perpetrator (for instance, showing that a hair found at the scene came from a suspect's head), a detective can *prove* that the perpetrator was at the scene of the crime!

Want to see what a magnet you are (and everybody else is!) for picking up trace evidence? Try this:

What You Do

1. Put on your clean, white socks and walk around your house a bit. How clean are your socks now?

2. Remove your socks and carefully examine them. Use your magnifying glass for an extra up-close look. Can you find any

evidence of the rooms you walked through? Any fibers from rugs? Any hairs? Any crumbs from the kitchen floor?

3. Take a piece of tape and fold it in a loop with the sticky side facing out. Stick the tape on the bottom of your socks. Put the socks on again, and walk around

the house one more time. Try to visit the same areas, with the tape, that you just went through without it. Did you pick up more stuff this time? Use your magnifying glass for a closer look. Can you identify additional trace evidence now?

4. Put on your shoes and pull the second pair of clean, white socks on *over them*. Go outside and walk around. Walk through a bunch of different places—the street, your front yard, some grass (if people stare, tell them you're breaking in your new socks!). Then take off your socks, come back inside, and ask your fellow rookie to examine your socks like you did before. Can he find evidence of where you walked? Can he tell from where each bit of trace evidence was picked up? Was there a difference in the type of evidence you picked up outside than inside?

What's the Real Deal?

Trace evidence is such an effective forensic tool because most people don't realize how much *junk* they cart around with them! For instance: Did you know that you lose between 50 to 100 hairs each day? Because we're constantly shedding, people often leave hairs all over the place!

When you come home from school or after a hard day playing outside, you will usually carry some evidence of your day on you. Stuck on the soles of your shoes, trapped in the fabric of your clothes, hidden under your fingernails—a tiny diary of your day's travels reveals itself. A skilled investigator can find this evidence—whether you pick it up at a crime scene or leave it behind. To a detective, the stuff that usually ends up in a vacuum cleaner can be a treasure trove of information!

◦De-feet-ed◦

Stuff You'll Need
• Shoe covers **DA**
• Talcum powder or baby powder

When a detective works a **crime scene**, she (and everyone else!) must be careful not to bring *more* **trace evidence** into the scene than was already there. Everyone picks up and drops off trace evidence all the time—it's unavoidable. If a detective isn't careful, she could end up investigating evidence that she (or another investigator!) brought there accidentally.

This is especially true with footprints. When investigating a crime, detectives walk through every inch of the crime scene, searching high and low for evidence. If they're not careful, it's easy for them to trample important clues at the scene, or leave new footprints of their own that will only confuse the investigation!

In order to make sure the crime scene is safe from those pesky feet of theirs, detectives wear special shoe covers, or "booties," over their feet while at a crime scene. Shoe covers don't just keep detectives from bringing trace evidence into a crime scene—they also make sure that detectives and the rest of the team working the scene don't mix their own footprints with any the **perpetrator** left. This can be very important—because a crime scene examination can include not only detectives, but a **CSI** team as well.

So break out your shoe covers, and get ready to take them for a spin!

What You Do

Since much of the trace evidence people leave behind comes from their shoes (because that's what's in contact with the ground, after all!), a good way to be sure not to leave evidence of *yourself* at a crime scene is by covering your shoes. Shoe covers seal a detective's shoes at a crime scene. As a rookie practicing your crime scene skills, you should do the same.

An important tip: Put the shoe covers on once you're *inside the crime scene*. If you put them on outside...well, you remember what those white socks looked like in *Case File #5: Without a Trace? I Don't Think So!* You don't want all that stuff walking into your secure area!

1. Head into a room with a shaggy carpet or rug. Wearing just your shoes, walk across it (make sure there aren't any other footprints already there!).

2. Slip on your shoe covers over your shoes and walk over the carpet again, next to the prints you just made. Can you see a

difference? Do the shoe covers leave any footprints at all?

3. Now, in your kitchen, sprinkle some of the talcum or baby powder in a thick layer on the floor in an area about the size of your teacher's desk at school (be sure to get the permission of a senior detective first!).

4. With just your shoes on (not the shoe covers), walk across the powder.

5. Now, put your shoe covers on and walk over the powder again, right next to the footprints you just left with your shoes only. Compare the two sets of footprints. Are they easy to tell apart? What differences do you notice?

6. Don't forget to sweep up the powder when you're done!

What's the Real Deal?

You should have seen from practicing with shoe covers that they will usually leave no footprint—or only a very slight one. In the cases where shoe covers leave a faint footprint, detectives working the case will easily be able to tell the difference between shoe cover prints and prints that are real evidence. The footprints you made with your shoes should have been pretty obvious: the ridges of the bottom of your shoes should have been easy to see in the baby powder and also (but probably less so) on the rug. The prints you made with the shoe covers should have been less obvious or even non-existent.

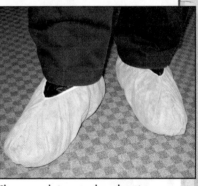

Shoe covers being worn by a detective at a crime scene.

Detectives and **CSI technicians** don't use shoe covers at every crime scene. For instance, at a crime at an outdoor location where lots of people walk every day, it's nearly impossible to know what footprints were made by the perpetrator and what ones were made by innocent bystanders—so why bother with shoe covers? The same goes for inside crime scenes that a lot of people have walked in *before* the investigation began (like a living room where there was a big party, for instance). In cases like those, a detective will have to focus on clues other than footprints to investigate the case.

Following the Footprints

Along with **fingerprints** and **trace evidence**, good clues can be gathered by examining footprints found at a **crime scene**, as long as they're not your own (as discovered in *Case File #6: De-feet-ed*).

By examining footprints, detectives can not only learn some things about the person who made them (shoe size, for instance), they can also make pretty good guesses about what that person is *like*. (Believe it or not, what we wear on our feet can say a lot about us!) Detectives use these guesses to help build a **theory** as to who the **perpetrator** is. Want to try it?

Stuff You'll Need

- A few rookie friends
- Shoes, sneakers, boots, and other footwear of all types
- Magnifying glass
- Ruler

What You Do

1. Invite some friends over and have each of them bring along a few different pairs of shoes.

2. Head outside and find some sand or soft dirt (snow works even better). Now, have each friend press their shoes down as hard as they can onto the ground (don't move the shoes around—just *press*).

3. After you and your friends have made footprints for all the footwear, take a close look at each print. Compare it to the actual shoe. How much alike is the shoe and the print? How different? For example: If the soles of one of the shoes is clogged with chewing gum—can you see that in the footprint? Some shoe soles have writing on them. Can you see any? Can you actually read the writing in the shoe's impression? On a real case, this would be an excellent clue!

4. Now have your friends put on one pair of their shoes and make footprints next to the ones they've just made with their hands. Using your magnifying glass, examine these new footprints closely. Compare them to the ones made by hand.

5. Take your ruler and measure how deep the footprints your friends made by hand are. Then measure how deep the footprints they made with their feet are. Usually, unless the ground is very hard, the footprints made by people wearing their shoes will be deeper. That's because when you walk normally, you press the ground harder than you do if you make prints by hand.

6. Using your ruler again, measure the depth of each of your friends' footprints. Is there a difference between them? If one person is heavier than another person, will their footprints be deeper or more shallow?

7. Now, examining the footprints, see if you can tell any of the following about the person from their footwear:
   • Their size or age?
   • Whether they are male or female?

What's the Real Deal?

Examining footprints is an important detective skill. By carefully studying footprints left at a crime scene, skilled detectives can often figure out not only the perpetrator's gender and age—they can also tell their *weight* and *height*. For example: If the footprint is very small, you know that the person is probably small. But does that *definitely* mean they are young? What if the footprint is of a grown woman with small feet? On the other hand, if the print is very big, it could be a young person who's big for their age. As for height, by measuring the distance between footprints from a person who is walking, skilled investigators can make a pretty good guess how long that person's legs are—and so how tall they are, as well! These are good clues—but like all clues, they need to be put together with *other* evidence before you have definite answers!

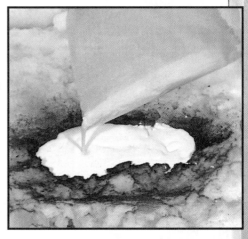

Because footprints have potential to be good clues, **CSI technicians** use a number of high-tech ways of recording them. Sensitive cameras placed over a footprint will record the tiniest details of a footprint. A special type of plaster can also be poured *into* the footprint, as shown in the photo here. After the plaster hardens, it's removed and cleaned—leaving a perfect representation of the print and all its details! That way, you're not just *finding* a footprint at a crime scene—you're hanging on to it as well!

Big Mouth!

You've seen how **fingerprints** and footprints work, now it's time to see if you can spot different types of "prints" at a **crime scene**—lip prints and tooth prints!

Believe it or not, these types of prints are different from person to person—so different, in fact, that if you find evidence of either of them at a crime scene, you can use it to help prove your suspect was there. As actually happens sometimes, a criminal may decide to take time out from committing a crime to get a drink or have a snack (like when they're burglarizing a house, for instance). In cases like that, a sharp detective can try to use lip and teeth prints from the scene to link that hungry or thirsty **perpetrator** to the crime!

Want to see how it works?

What You Do

Part I. Read My Lips!

It may surprise you, but lip prints can—in some cases—be as good a piece of evidence as fingerprints. Just like with fingerprints, lip prints have certain grooves and tiny markings that are unique to every person (you can see them, if you look *real close* in a mirror!). And like fingerprints, these lip patterns don't change as you get older. If you find a good enough lip print at the crime scene, those grooves and markings should be visible—and so, a possible match for a suspect!

1. Get some glasses from your kitchen. Try to pick ones that are different colors and made of different materials (like clear glass or blue plastic). Line them up in your room and wipe them clean with a cloth.

2. Step out into the hallway while your friend gets busy putting his lip prints on a few of the glasses (but not all of them).
Tell him to act like he's taking a sip of water from them.

3. When he's done, inspect each glass with your magnifying glass. Can you figure out which glasses he "drank" from? Is there a difference between the prints on the different-colored glasses?

4. Now swap roles and see if your friend can identify which glasses you drank from!

Tip:
Try applying lipstick or lip balm before leaving a lip print on a drinking glass.

Part II. To Tell the Tooth!
Some foods—especially soft ones—will show a pretty clear outline of your teeth after you

bite into them. A soft apple or a hunk of cheese will often leave enough of an impression of teeth that detectives can sometimes use these prints to match to a suspect in a case. Just like with footprints, **CSI technicians** can even make a cast of the teeth prints by pouring plaster into the prints, then letting the plaster harden before removing it. Now they've got a permanent record of that bite!

1. First, make sure that the cheese you're using is your own! Don't just bite into any hunk of cheese from your refrigerator without the permission of a senior detective!

2. In a thick part of the cheese, open wide and take a big bite! You don't have to swallow, if you're not a cheese-lover!

3. Now examine the marks left by your teeth on the cheese. Do you see the impressions your teeth made?

4. Look at your teeth in the mirror. Can you match any of the marks your teeth made in the cheese with the way your teeth look? Are you missing any teeth in front? Did they leave a mark in the cheese?

5. Have your rookie friend take a bite in another piece of cheese and compare her bite mark to yours. How different are they?

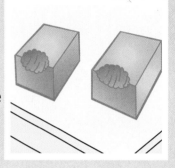

What's the Real Deal?

Lip prints and teeth prints can sometimes provide good clues. For instance, if the lip prints on a glass have lipstick on them, then detectives know they're probably looking for a woman. If the tooth prints show a missing tooth or one that seems to have a crooked bite, that can tell them something about how the perpetrator looks.

But lip and teeth prints aren't *just* found at a crime scene where a perpetrator stopped for a snack. Imagine you're investigating a bank **robbery** in which the perpetrator got away by car. You discover the car abandoned a few miles away, and decide to check it out for clues. In the back seat, you discover a soda bottle with a lip print on it, and a half-eaten apple. Because a perpetrator decided to have lunch while fleeing the scene, you've now got yourself some solid clues!

As you probably noticed, this type of evidence isn't always easy to see. With lip prints, a lot depends on the color of the glass the perpetrator used, and if a female perpetrator was wearing lipstick or not. And for teeth prints, a lot depends on what the perpetrator was eating. But as a detective examining a crime scene, don't forget to check for these unusual clues. They could just help solve the case!

P.S. Lip prints and teeth prints are little used by detectives in the United States, but they can be additional evidence to help put together a case, as well as useful tools to experiment with.

Stuff You'll Need
- Magnifying glass 🛡️DA
- A few rookie friends
- Tape
- Some sheets of plain white paper
- Pen

Got a Match?

You know, **perpetrators** can often be very careless—and that's a good thing—for a detective! Since perpetrators almost always leave some evidence behind when they commit crimes, detectives usually have some good clues to work with. But sometimes, a really careless perpetrator will leave *more* than just prints or **trace evidence**—and that can make the detective's life easier!

When a detective finds a whole *object* that a perpetrator has left at a **crime scene**, the key becomes to *link* it to a suspect—that is, to find a way to prove that it belonged to the perpetrator. If you can show that a piece of clothing or a burglar's tool found at a crime scene belongs to a particular person, well, you've probably found yourself a suspect!

Try this matching activity with your friends. It's not exactly how you match evidence to a perp in a real crime scene, but it *will* give you an idea about how it works.

What You Do

1. First, use your magnifying glass to carefully examine the clothes you're wearing. Look at your shirt, for instance, on the outside and inside of the collar. Do you see any hairs or other stuff?

2. Invite some fellow rookies over and have them bring their jackets. Throw all the jackets together on a bed or sofa.

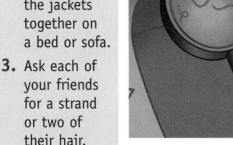

3. Ask each of your friends for a strand or two of their hair. Keep each rookie's hair sample separate! To do this, tape the hairs on sheets of paper so you can keep track of them. Use a separate sheet for each of your friends and write their names on their sheets.

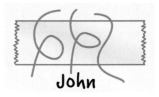

John

4. Now, using your magnifying glass, pick up one of the jackets from the bed. Examine it closely for stray hairs. Can you match it to one of your friend's hair samples? The collar is a good place to start, but don't forget to check inside the sleeves, if you need to! If you *can* find a hair on a jacket that looks the same as one of the hair samples, then you've got a match! See if you can match up each of the jackets to its correct owner, just by looking at the hair samples.

Olivia

What's the Real Deal?

To a detective, an object found at a crime scene can be a great clue. But it's only as good as *the detective's* ability to find its owner. Trace evidence and **fingerprints** are an excellent way to find a match. The ability to match an object from a crime scene to a particular perpetrator, however, especially in the absence of clear trace evidence, can be a difficult challenge faced by a detective. With so many products, like jackets, mass-produced and often with brand names sold across the country, it can be hard to find a clue that can only belong to one person. After all—how many Gap jean jackets are floating around out there? But there's *one* mass-produced object of the modern age that's a major exception.

Today, the explosion of cell phones has provided countless detectives with clues they've used to track down perpetrators. Because most cell phones have phone numbers stored in them (including the number of the phone's owner), cell phones have helped investigators find perpetrators who've left their phones in getaway cars, dropped them while fleeing, or simply put them down at a crime scene and forgotten to pick them up again! Check out this section's *Case in Point* for an incredible example of a case involving the careless use of a cell phone.

If you're lucky enough to find a cell phone at the scene, too—or instead of other trace evidence or fingerprints—matching it to your perpetrator can be just a phone call away!

CASE IN POINT

Hello? Can Someone Come Arrest Me, Please?

In June of 2003, a man in Hicksville, NY, was arrested for committing a burglary at the house of one of his neighbors. It was an easy arrest—the detectives had a "taped confession." Sort of....

Before committing the crime, the perpetrator, a 19-year old man, used his cell phone to call the victim—making sure that the house was empty. During the break-in, the perpetrator accidentally hit the "redial" button on his phone—causing it to call the victim's house again! When the victim didn't answer, the call went to his voice mail—where the entire crime was recorded! Later, the perpetrator could be heard on the voice mail talking to his accomplice—the person he was committing the crime with. After, when the victim listened to his voice mail and heard the crime, not only did he recognize the voice of his neighbor, but the two perpetrators called each other by name on the recorded message and discussed which stuff to steal!

The perps were tracked down by police, arrested, and charged with burglary.

33

Stuff You'll Need
• An open mind

Testing: One, Two, Three

A detective arriving at a **crime scene** can be a bit like going into a theater after the movie's started. There's a lot of interesting stuff going on, but you're not really sure what it means yet!

Once at the crime scene, a detective has to begin to try to make sense of all the evidence that she's presented with. One of the best ways to do this is to develop a **theory**—an educated guess about how the crime occurred. By looking at all the evidence you have and imagining how it might fit together, you can often come up with a pretty good idea about what happened, and who did it. With a theory, you're never *sure*—you're just taking an idea and testing it out!

For instance, let's say you have a crime scene at a house where a safe was **burglarized**. There are two sets of footprints, but only one of these sets goes into the house—the other set stops outside, by the front door. In this case, you might develop a theory that there were *two* **perpetrators**—one of whom worked on the safe, while the other stood outside and acted as a lookout. Now, according to this theory, you have to consider the idea that you're looking for a burglary *team*! But as with all theories—you could be wrong, and there could be another explanation. So you have to still be open to other possibilities!

Want to try to develop some theories?

What You Do

Part I. Query...With a Theory!

Here is a picture of the kitchen of someone who lives on a high-level floor in a very large apartment building. While the owner of the apartment was out of the house from 12:00 p.m. to 12:30 p.m., somebody broke in and took $3,000 in savings from a bag stuffed into the back of the kitchen cabinet above the refrigerator. The apartment building has its own security service, janitors, gardeners, and a 24-hour doorman on duty. When you interview the doorman, he says that he didn't see any strangers go in or out of the building all day. Can you come up with

a theory as to who the perpetrator might be? Check out *Case Closed* to see if you're right.

34

Part II. Two's Company...
Theories a Crowd!

Sometimes when a crime scene is very big or there's a lot of evidence, a whole *team* of three or four detectives will respond to the scene! And a whole lot of detectives can mean a whole lot of theories!

In fact, even in cases where one detective responds, if there's a lot of evidence or the crime scene is difficult to "read," there could be a number of different theories for the crime. When there's more than one theory on a case, it's the job of the **lead investigator** to decide which one fits the evidence best!

Test this out:

1. Look at the scene here. It's in the library of a rich man who lives alone in a mansion. Now, imagine you and two other detectives have been called to the scene to investigate a very "heavy" burglary from the man's safe—a million-dollar gold necklace! After interviewing the old man, you discover the following:

   • The man recently had an argument with his son. The son had been living with him, but he moved out a week ago.

   • The man recently took out an expensive insurance policy on the necklace, so that if anything ever happened to the piece, he'd be repaid the full amount of what it's worth.

   • The man had a safe installed at home a month ago to protect the necklace.

2. After considering the evidence at this crime scene, and what you know about the case—can you come up with *more than one* theory of what might have happened here, and who might have done it? Check out *Case Closed* to see some possible theories.

What's the Real Deal?

From viewing these cases and accompanying illustrations and testing out your theories on how to solve them, you should have learned one major rule: No theory is perfect! While it may seem obvious what occurred at a particular crime scene, it's always important to keep an open mind. Almost any crime scene can support a number of different theories, if you think hard enough.

That's why a whole lot of detectives can mean not only a whole lot of theories—but a whole lot of arguments, too! Detectives have been known to disagree on the correct theory for a crime, but healthy disagreement is useful. By discussing the case and comparing points, they learn from each other and test various theories out, until the lead investigator eventually finds the one that fits!

On the Lighter Side

As you've seen, the detective's world is a hidden world. Much of what occupies a detective's day involves looking for things that most people can't see—such as trace evidence and fingerprints. And more and more in the modern age, detectives get help seeing what's hidden by using *technology*. Today, advances in research and equipment have improved forensic science so much, it's amazing anyone would choose a life of crime!

A good example of this is UV lighting. UV (short for "ultraviolet") lighting is a special form of light that makes some things that are less visible in normal light suddenly show up clearly. For instance, imagine you have a case that centers on a piece of writing—a legal document like a will. If you suspect that someone tried to change the writing on the will, you could try to prove it with UV lighting. By shining the UV light on the document and looking at it carefully, the original writing would show through!

But UV lighting is valuable for looking at more than writing: very thin scratches or shallow grooves that have been made in paper, wood, or metal will often show up best under UV light. This is a great help to a detective trying to figure out if a lock on a house or car has been picked. Because lock picks are very thin and made of metal (like metallic toothpicks), they will usually leave very tiny scratch marks on a lock or doorknob. UV lighting can make these nearly invisible scratches, known as tool marks, become more visible.

Want to see some UV magic?

What You Do

Part I. The Write Stuff!

1. First, using the blue pen, write your name on a piece of white paper.

2. Then, using the black permanent marker, write your name again, *directly over* what you just wrote in blue. Try to write your name exactly the same as the first time. Can you see your original writing?

3. Now, take your UV light, and shine it on what you just wrote. Can you see your original blue writing *now*? Can you see the pen impressions? Try turning the light off in the room where you are. Is it easier to see the impression the original blue pen made on your paper? If a detective saw that impression, he would know that under the black magic marker is something that was written *first*!

Part II. Scratch That!

If it's scratches you're after, UV light can be an effective tool here, too. Shine it on a surface that looks smooth—and if there's scrapes or tool marks there, they'll be much more visible (they show up even better if you use your UV light together with your magnifying glass).

1. Take a close look at a lock in your house —the one in your front door, for example. Shine your UV light on it to see if you can find any scratches.

2. Now, let's try something else. Place the paper over the dark-colored notebook or book. Write something on the paper. Remove the paper and get down close to the book. Shine your UV light on the surface of the book. Do you see any impressions? You should see the impression you just made. Use your magnifying glass to really make things clearer!

More From Detective Squad

Log on to www.scholastic.com/detective for more UV fun!

JUST THE FACTS

Investigators use UV lights (like the one you received this month, but much more powerful) to illuminate crime scenes and documents. UV lighting, for example, is one of the best ways to detect counterfeit money. Today's bills have special inks and marks that show up only under UV light. If these don't show— it's funny money!

Investigators also use very powerful UV lighting to detect art forgery. Modern paints glow under UV light, because of all the chemicals used when mixing the paint. But paint used by the "Old Masters" hundreds of years ago doesn't glow. So if someone tries to sell you the Mona Lisa, and it glows under UV light—forget it!

The same is true for paper products. Modern paper has chemical bleaches and dyes in it that glow under UV light. Old paper (before 1950 or so) doesn't. So if it doesn't glow—it's old!

Using these dating techniques, investigators can discover fake antiques, homemade money, "historical" documents that were printed yesterday—all sorts of scams and flim-flams designed to separate the unsuspecting from their money!

What's the Real Deal?

After shining your UV light on the writing in *Part I* and the grooves you made on the book cover in *Part II*, you should have seen how UV lighting can help you bring out small marks and indentations that are less visible. What you did here is the same as looking for hidden writing on a **robbery** note or looking for tool marks on a picked lock. It's an important skill—and a great example of how technology helps detectives find even the smallest clues!

You should have seen some scratches on your lock in *Part II*. Does that mean your lock has been picked and your house broken into? No! All locks will have *some* scratches on them, unless they're brand new. These aren't made by robbers, just by everyday use. If the lock *had* been picked, you would have seen more obvious scratches inside the keyhole.

DET. HIGH-TECH!

DNA

Today, new developments in computers, photography, chemistry, and other sciences have made detective work more advanced than ever. But there's one development that beats them all—DNA.

In every cell of your body, a super-tiny code exists that tells your body how to grow (think of it like the plans for building a new house or the instructions for putting a bike together—except more complicated!). These tiny plans determine who you are, and—just like fingerprints—everybody's are different. But the big advantage of DNA is that, because it's in *every* cell of your body, forensic scientists can get it from any bodily trace evidence— your hair, your toothbrush, even the saliva in your mouth!

Using DNA analysis, detectives can now prove a perpetrator was at the scene if he so much as sheds a single hair while there. The DNA taken from the hair strand can be matched to the DNA of a suspect—and you've got your perpetrator!

DNA is such a new technology that its use in police work is still being explored. But there's no doubt that it's the future of forensic science. You'll be learning more about DNA in other *Detective Academy* books. As a detective, DNA is one of the best tools you've got!

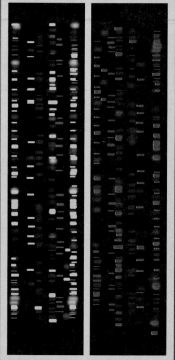

On a special computer program, DNA can be blown up and studied up close (see below). Above, two different strands of DNA are compared.

Gotcha!

Believe it or not, rookie, sometimes as a detective there will be a case when you *know* who the **perpetrator** is...but you can't prove it! Even though in your gut your experience is telling you that a certain suspect is guilty, you may not have enough evidence to prove you're right. Other times, you may have your list of suspects narrowed down to two or three people—but you can't figure out *which* of them is guilty! In cases like these, you can use some tricks of the trade to get your man (or woman!).

Want to see how?

Stuff You'll Need
- A dollar bill
- UV powder [DA]
- A wallet or purse
- Some rookie friends
- UV light [DA]
- Pencil [DA]
- A few sheets of paper
- A green or dark-colored folder or large envelope

What You Do

Part I. Light-Fingered!

1. First, take the dollar bill and sprinkle it *very lightly* with your UV powder. Then put it back in your wallet.

2. Next, tell your fellow rookies that you're such a great detective, you'll be able to catch anyone who tries to steal from you! Leave your wallet in the room and step outside—but before you do, instruct your friends that *one* of them should steal the dollar bill from your wallet while you're gone. Bet them you'll be able to catch the perpetrator.

3. When you return to the room, ask to see all your friends' hands. Shine the UV light on their fingertips. The one whose fingers glow is your perp!

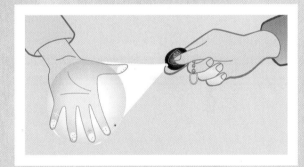

Part II. File Under...Caught!

1. Invite a different group of friends over than the ones you used in *Part I*. Write each of their names on separate sheets of paper and put the sheets in a folder or envelope. Then, sprinkle a *very light* dusting of UV powder on the folder (since your powder is green, a green colored folder would work best, but another dark color should be okay, too) and leave it someplace in your room,

out in the open. Do this while your friends wait in another room.

2. Tell your friends to come into the room where you are. Say that you've been investigating some recent **burglaries** in which the perpetrator snooped around inside people's houses. Say that you've been making notes about the case, and that you keep these notes in the folder. Tell them that even though the police are stumped, *you* know that the culprit is one of your friends in this very room—and that you have all the proof you need to put the perp away!

3. Before you leave the room for a few minutes, tell your friends to decide among themselves while you're gone who is the guilty one. That person is the one who should check the folder when you're out of the room to see if you fingered the right perp.

4. When you return, ask all your friends to step forward and show you their hands. Shine your UV light on their fingertips. Whoever's fingertips are glowing is guilty. Pronounce the case solved!

SPOTLIGHT ON
THE FBI LABORATORY

Hey, rookie—ever wonder what you would do if you were working on a case, but found yourself...stumped?

Even in a case where there's a lot of evidence, there are times when detectives simply can't fit all the pieces of the puzzle together. But if the case has a lot of physical evidence—trace evidence, fingerprints, footprints, and so on—one of the things a detective *can* do is send this evidence to be analyzed at the FBI Laboratory.

Located in Quantico, Virginia, the Laboratory at the Federal Bureau of Investigation is the most advanced crime analysis lab in America—and probably the world! All the latest technology for analyzing evidence is available there, including super-powerful microscopes, computers, a chemistry lab, photograph and sound equipment, and more. The FBI employees who staff the lab are highly experienced experts in their field.

Police departments all over America—and sometimes even in other countries—send tough-to-analyze evidence to the FBI for help. For instance, in 1996, police in Scotland sent a single hair all the way to Virginia to be analyzed by the FBI. That analysis eventually led the Scottish police to solve a homicide (which is a term for when one person kills another)!

The FBI Lab conducts more than *one million* exams each year! If you would like to read more about the Lab, you can log on to the FBI website at **http://www.fbi.gov/hq/lab/labhome.htm**. Click on it to see what the latest technology and techniques are for analyzing crime scene evidence. It's a great resource for detectives in training!

What's the Real Deal?

In this activity, you should have seen how it's possible for a detective to trick a perpetrator by outsmarting him. Did your friends fall for the traps you set? Were they surprised when you caught them? Bet they were *green* with embarrassment!

To really trap someone, however, a detective needs to have a pretty good idea who the perpetrator is in the first place, or where he'll strike next. After all, it's pretty tough to trick a burglar when you have no idea which house he's going to break into next!

For that reason, trapping the perpetrator is much easier if you know where to find him—and if you can guess what he's going to do! Take a look at the *Case in Point* below for a good example of how a detective set a clever trap for a perpetrator who was already under arrest!

CASE IN POINT Thirst Quencher

In early 2000, New York City police arrested a man for a minor theft—and wound up with much more than they bargained for!

After the arrest, detectives developed information that the perpetrator might be a man they were looking for in a series of serious assaults. What was needed was a DNA sample to prove it—but the perpetrator refused to give police so much as a strand of hair!

So detectives decided to trick him. While still in jail, the perpetrator was offered a drink of water and got one—in a paper cup. After he threw the cup away in a garbage can, the suspect was removed from the cell to be processed on the theft arrest. While he was gone, detectives retrieved the cup from the garbage can so that the traces of saliva on the cup could be tested for DNA.

The trick worked, and based on the DNA evidence, the man was later charged with the more serious crimes!

On the Job: At Work with CSI Technician David Sentowski

Dave Sentowski, NYPD CSI tech, ready for work.

As a **CSI technician**, Officer David Sentowski of the New York Police Department (NYPD) has seen his share of **crime scenes**. "Every one of them is different," Dave says. "It's one of the things I like about the job. It keeps you interested."

Dave on the road, heading to a crime scene.

Like most investigators, Dave started out as a **first responder**, patrolling the city streets. That's where he learned the job and got interested in working crime scenes.

But it wasn't until he saw a CSI team at work on a "heavy" (complicated) crime scene that he knew the work was for him. "I had never really paid much attention to how the evidence guys did their work. Then, I responded to a robbery scene that had every kind of evidence you could think of. Blood drops, footprints, **fingerprints**—you name it. And I watched as the crime scene team went over every square inch of it. By the time they and the detectives were done, they knew *exactly* what had occurred. I was fascinated." After five years working in uniform, Dave got his transfer to working crime scenes!

Dave's equipment van.

Very often, the "graveyard" shift (midnight to 8 a.m.) is the busiest for police departments—many serious crimes occur late at night. Dave received this shift after requesting it, and he was assigned to work in one of the busiest areas of New York City: Manhattan.

Dave's "day" starts at about 11:00 p.m., when he arrives at work and goes to his locker to change into his "work clothes." The trousers that Dave wears have a lot of extra pockets—these are good for holding plastic gloves, fingerprint powder, and other special equipment that he needs throughout his shift.

Getting ready to process a crime scene.

Soon after midnight, Dave and his partner are in their van, driving Manhattan's streets and listening to the police radio. The back of their van is so loaded down with crime scene equipment that the backseats had to be removed to make more space!

One of Dave's many equipment cases!

Unlike some other police departments that may not be as busy, the NYPD keeps their evidence teams "on the road"—that is, driving around and waiting to be called to a crime scene by radio. That way, they can be at the scene at a moment's notice!

After he's worked one crime scene, Dave's off to another job.

At 2:35 a.m., a call comes in; there's been a **burglary** in an apartment building, and Dave and his partner are being paged. Dave gets on the radio. "10-4, Central," he tells the **emergency dispatcher**. "We're responding to the scene."

CSI equipment, including powders, lights, and tape.

At the crime scene, Dave and his partner talk to the first responders and the detective, getting the story. Then they decide where they should start their search. First step: dusting for prints. Dave works on the doorknob to one of the rooms, while his partner checks around outside the apartment, looking to see if the **perpetrator** dropped anything as he fled.

After an hour or so, Dave and his partner have a couple of good prints, including a **partial** off the doorknob. They then take what's called an "elimination print" of the apartment's owner. "The victim's prints will be all over the apartment," Dave says. "With the elimination print, we can then make sure that the prints we've found don't just belong to the victim."

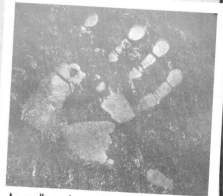
An excellent palm print lifted at the scene of a crime.

By the time the night is over, Dave and his partner will go to two more crime scenes, including another burglary. "Like I said, every scene is different," says Dave as his shift ends. "Every time we respond, I wonder what we're getting into. And that's what keeps it challenging!"

Case of the Missing Briefcase

Well rookie, by now you should have a pretty good feel for what goes on at a **crime scene**. You've seen how detectives can use **fingerprints**, **trace evidence**, and **footprints** found at a scene to develop a **theory** of who the **perpetrator** is. And in your *Basic Training Manual*, you learned about motive and interviewing suspects.

Before you move on to future books in the *Detective Academy* series (and even more new skills and gadgets!), it's always a good idea to practice what you've learned so far.

So here's a case for you to chew on, based on an actual crime. Can you put all of what you learned together now to solve this crime? Take your time and study it closely. You've caught this case, rookie, so use all your abilities as a detective—and close it out!

In June of 1997, a detective was called to a New York elementary school by **patrol** officers who had responded to the scene of a 10-36. The detective was informed that an English teacher, Mr. McSwiggan, returned to the English teachers' office after the last class of the day, where he discovered his briefcase missing from his desk. After making sure there was no perpetrator in the vicinity, the **first responders** called for a detective.

After arriving at the scene, the detective interviewed Mr. McSwiggan, who told him, "I had a lot of important stuff in that briefcase. I had school stuff like tests and this year's final grades, and I had my house keys and car keys. I also had my wallet, which had not

only money, but four different credit cards! I really need to find that case!"

When the detective asked Mr. McSwiggan to tell the story of how he discovered his briefcase missing, the teacher said that after teaching his last class, he went to the English teachers' office to collect his things. Before he entered the office, he met Jennifer Gooden, who was waiting to talk to him about forming a chess club. The detective then asked Mr. McSwiggan about Jennifer Gooden. "She's one of the best students in the school,"

Mr. McSwiggan said. "She's been slacking off a bit lately, I don't know why. But she's our brightest. She's even applied to a high school for gifted children."

The detective then interviewed Jennifer Gooden, who said that just before Mr. McSwiggan arrived, she saw Frankie Malvo, another student, coming out of the teachers' office alone. She said he was holding a large shopping bag and walking very fast.

"Yes, that boy—he's often in trouble for disobeying teachers and talking in class," Mr. McSwiggan said. "In fact, he's probably in detention right now. I'll go get him."

Around that time, **CSI** arrived to check the scene. CSI and the detective entered the secured crime scene area.

CSI dusted for prints around Mr. McSwiggan's desk and looked for trace evidence. They discovered some size 9 footprints outside the office window, as if somebody had been standing there looking in, and some red hairs on the top of the desk. They also photographed footprints found on the office floor.

Then Mr. McSwiggan returned with Frankie Malvo, who had been sitting in detention. When the detective interviewed him, Frankie was very uncooperative, saying, "Yeah, I was in that hallway. So what? I was running because I was late for detention. And the only bag I had was my own book bag."

CSI then checked Frankie Malvo's shoes against the footprints found on the office floor, but stated they didn't look like a match. "These prints seem to come from about a size 5 sneaker, possibly female."

"Well, *of course* they do, sir," Jennifer Gooden suddenly said, rolling her eyes. "They're probably *mine*. Like I said, I was here waiting for Mr. McSwiggan to arrive, so we could talk about the chess club."

The detective next interviewed the school janitor, who admitted he had been in the teachers' office near the end of the school day, but denied knowing anything about the briefcase. Before the **theft** was discovered, he had just finished his normal routine of cleaning up and emptying the garbage cans in the office and then set to work on waxing the hallway. When questioned, the janitor stated, "Yes, while I was running the wax machine, I caught a glimpse of that Frankie kid as he ran out of the hallway into the stairway. I remember that now."

"Was he carrying anything?" the detective asked.

"Yes, he had a big bag of some sort."

Then the detective asked the janitor what size shoe he wears. "Size 9," the janitor said.

With all the interviews done, CSI gave the detective a final rundown of their findings:

- The footprints outside the window appeared to match the janitor's shoes.
- Some of the fingerprints found around Mr. McSwiggan's desk were child-sized.
- The red hairs found near the desk appeared to match the janitor's hair.
- The dirt found near Mr. McSwiggan's desk in the office appeared to come from school grounds—and matched dirt on the janitor's shoes.

So rookie, considering the evidence, the suspects, and the motive each suspect had (remember motive, from your *Basic Training Manual*?), can you catch this perpetrator? Check out *Case Closed* to see if you're right.

💻 Want another case to solve? You'll find one at **www.scholastic.com/detective**. Log on!

CASE ⊙ CLOSED
(Answer Key)

(page 9)
Detectives mostly deal with crimes that are in the "twenties"—that is, crimes in the *past*, not the present. With these crimes, the perpetrator is already gone, and an investigation needs to start in order to find the suspect.

Case File #1: Radio Active! (pages 11–12)
Part II.

1. "Central, we've got a 10-39 here, corner of Broadway and Canal. Two injuries, not life threatening. Roll me a bus."

   Translation: *"Dispatcher, we have a vehicle accident here, at the corner of Broadway and Canal Street. Two people are hurt, but their lives are not in danger. Please send an ambulance."*

2. "Units, I've got a call of a 10-25 at 325 Owen Avenue. Caller states perp is 10-87. Unit in the area to advise?"

   This is the emergency dispatcher talking to the uniformed police officers on patrol! It translates as: *"First responders, there is a 9-1-1 call of a past robbery at 325 Owen Avenue. The victim says that the perpetrator has left the scene. Is there a first responding patrol officer in the area to go to this scene?"*

3. "Receiving a call of a 10-38, East 10th Street and Nicholls Boulevard. Caller states perp is still 10-97. Repeat, perp is 97 on this 10-38. Unit available to respond?"

   This is the emergency dispatcher talking again! It means: *"There is a 9-1-1 call of a vehicle theft in*

CASE CLOSED

progress. The perpetrator is still on the scene. Repeat, the perpetrator is still there. Is there a patrol officer in the area to respond to the scene?"

Case File #1: *Part III.*

Dispatcher: *Patrol officers, there is a 9-1-1 call of a burglary in progress. A burglary in progress at 425 North 47th Street, Apartment 4-B. The victim says that the perpetrator is a white male, approximately 35 years old, wearing blue jeans, black jacket, backward baseball cap. The victim says that he returned to his apartment and found the perpetrator in his kitchen. The victim says that the perpetrator threatened him. The victim didn't have any information on any weapons in the perpetrator's possession. The perpetrator is still on the scene. Repeat, the perpetrator is still there.*

Police Officer #1: *I understand that transmission, radio dispatcher, and I'll respond. Can you also radio for another patrol officer to go to that scene? Have another patrol officer go there, too, dispatcher, to back me up.*

Dispatcher: *I understand, I will do that.*

Police Officer #2: *Radio dispatcher, I'm already at the location of that burglary in progress. Send me an ambulance, please. The victim is an elderly man, and the perpetrator startled him. I want to make sure the victim is okay. Also, the perpetrator has left the scene. He left through the kitchen window.*

Dispatcher: *I understand. I will radio for an ambulance to respond to the scene. Patrol officers in the field, the perpetrator of this burglary has left the scene. I'm going to repeat the description of him. He's a male, white, approximately 35 years of age, wearing a—*

Police Officer #1: *I've got him spotted, radio dispatcher! Perpetrator just jumped off of the fire escape and is fleeing northbound on Eighth Avenue! North on Eighth Avenue. I'm chasing him. I need help right away! Help right away!*

Case File #2: Respond...and React!
(pages 13–15)

Here's what you should do when responding to this crime scene in each of these pictures:

Picture #1: Did you notice the fleeing perp? Even if you did, the first thing you should do here is make sure the elderly man is okay. Ask him if he needs an ambulance.

Once you've done that, *then* you can get on to your other duties: finding out what happened, radioing for assistance to chase that fleeing perp, securing the crime scene, and getting a detective over there fast!

Picture #2: The *first* thing you should do here is arrest that perpetrator! As a first responder, it's your job to get to emergencies as fast as you can. If the perp is there when you arrive— arrest him before he can flee!

Picture #3: This is a tough one. Because there's nobody visible, you might think to just secure the scene first. But wait: What if the perp is still hiding on the scene? What if someone is injured in

another room? The first thing you should do is make sure the perp isn't still there and that no one needs assistance in another room. Then secure the area, and get a detective. Remember to include *all* the evidence you see when securing the area.

Case File #3: Secure That Scene! (pages 16–18)

Part II. As you, rookie, already know but your friends may not, once you've made sure the crime scene is safe, and nobody needs your assistance—it's time to call for a detective! As a first responder, your job is pretty much done. Once the detective arrives and you tell him what happened—just step aside and let that detective do his thing!

CASE CLOSED (continued)

Case File #10: Testing: One, Two, Three (pages 34–35)

Part I. What's your theory? How about that the gardener did it—hence the muddy prints and the fact that no strangers were seen coming or going. As someone who works in the apartment building, the gardener would also know when the owner of the apartment left—essential, since the owner was only gone for a short time.

Part II. Here are a couple different theories:

1. The son did it. That's why nothing else in the room is disturbed. He knew where the safe was and knew how to get it open. From living in the house, he must have found out the safe combination somehow.

2. Somebody from the safe-company did it. They installed the safe, so they knew where it was and they had the combination. Again, that's why nothing else in the room was disturbed, and that's how they got the safe open.

3. The old man himself did it for the insurance money.

Case of the Missing Briefcase (pages 44–46)

Let's look at the suspects.

Frankie Malvo: While Frankie may be no angel, there's no evidence that he's a thief. Even Mr. McSwiggan says that Frankie only gets into trouble for "talking in class" and "disobeying teachers." Plus, there's no *physical* evidence that Frankie did it—no footprints or trace evidence. Only the "child-sized" fingerprints could have been his—but we don't know this for sure yet.

The janitor: We learn that emptying the trash in the office is part of his "routine," so we know that he's often in the office. And as the janitor, he works all around the school, so of course he will track some dirt from the school grounds into the office—and leave some red hairs as well! Just because he's left some trace evidence there, that doesn't mean he's the perpetrator—he works there! Even his footprints outside

the window don't mean anything. Remember, what else do janitors do? They wash windows!

That leaves: **Jennifer Gooden**. Well, did you catch Jennifer's lie? Jennifer first claimed that she had waited for Mr. McSwiggan outside the office—but when CSI stated that the footprints looked "female," she jumped in and said she had been *inside* the office. She *knew* her shoes would be a match—so she tried to cover it. As a detective, any witness who lies to you has to immediately become a suspect!

Now that we know Jennifer lied, a lot of the other evidence falls into place: the "child-sized fingerprints" found around the desk might normally have been useless, because as we learned in *Case File #4—Read the Fine Prints*, fingerprints found at a scene are only good if they can be matched to "on file" fingerprints—and what school children have their prints on file? But with Jennifer now a suspect, her prints could be checked against those found on the desk quite easily!

But what was Jennifer's *motive*? Why would an excellent student like her steal a briefcase? Well, do you remember what Mr. McSwiggan said was in his bag? *The final grades for the school year.* We also know that: (1) Jennifer hasn't been doing that well in school lately, and (2) She applied to a high school for gifted students. So with Jennifer's grades dropping lately, and with her applying to a special school—maybe she doesn't want this year's grades to be recorded!

In fact, that *was* Jennifer's motive. Frankie Malvo *had* run down the hall, carrying his own book bag. But as Jennifer exited the teachers' office with the briefcase, Frankie startled her, so she ditched it. Mr. McSwiggan arrived moments later. Jennifer almost got away with it!

Later, the detective found Mr. McSwiggan's briefcase in a garbage can at the end of the hall, near the door to the teachers' office—right where Jennifer had quickly stashed it. (Everything was still in it—Jennifer hadn't had time to remove anything!) After being caught lying, and presented with the evidence against her, Jennifer broke down and made a full confession. Case closed!